THE JPS B'NAI MITZVAH TORAH COMMENTARY

Metsora' (Leviticus 14:1–15:33)
Haftarah (2 Kings 7:3–20)

Rabbi Jeffrey K. Salkin

The Jewish Publication Society · Philadelphia
University of Nebraska Press · Lincoln

INTRODUCTION

News flash: the most important thing about becoming bar or bat mitzvah isn't the party. Nor is it the presents. Nor even being able to celebrate with your family and friends—as wonderful as those things are. Nor is it even standing before the congregation and reading the prayers of the liturgy—as important as that is.

No, the most important thing about becoming bar or bat mitzvah is sharing Torah with the congregation. And why is that? Because of all Jewish skills, that is the most important one.

Here is what is true about rites of passage: you can tell what a culture values by the tasks it asks its young people to perform on their way to maturity. In American culture, you become responsible for driving, responsible for voting, and yes, responsible for drinking responsibly.

In some cultures, the rite of passage toward maturity includes some kind of trial, or a test of strength. Sometimes, it is a kind of "outward bound" camping adventure. Among the Maasai tribe in Africa, it is traditional for a young person to hunt and kill a lion. In some Hispanic cultures, fifteen year-old girls celebrate the *quinceañera*, which marks their entrance into maturity.

What is Judaism's way of marking maturity? It combines both of these rites of passage: *responsibility* and *test*. You show that you are on your way to becoming a *responsible* Jewish adult through a public *test* of strength and knowledge—reading or chanting Torah, and then teaching it to the congregation.

This is the most important Jewish ritual mitzvah (commandment), and that is how you demonstrate that you are, truly, bar or bat mitzvah—old enough to be responsible for the mitzvot.

What Is Torah?

So, what exactly is the Torah? You probably know this already, but let's review.

The Torah (teaching) consists of "the five books of Moses," sometimes also called the *chumash* (from the Hebrew word *chameish,* which means "five"), or, sometimes, the Greek word Pentateuch (which means "the five teachings").

Here are the five books of the Torah, with their common names and their Hebrew names.

> **Genesis (The beginning), which in Hebrew is Bere'shit (from the first words—"When God began to create").** Bere'shit spans the years from Creation to Joseph's death in Egypt. Many of the Bible's best stories are in Genesis: the creation story itself; Adam and Eve in the Garden of Eden; Cain and Abel; Noah and the Flood; and the tales of the Patriarchs and Matriarchs, Abraham, Isaac, Jacob, Sarah, Rebekah, Rachel, and Leah. It also includes one of the greatest pieces of world literature, the story of Joseph, which is actually the oldest complete novel in history, comprising more than one-quarter of all Genesis.

> **Exodus (Getting out), which in Hebrew is Shemot (These are the names).** Exodus begins with the story of the Israelite slavery in Egypt. It then moves to the rise of Moses as a leader, and the Israelites' liberation from slavery. After the Israelites leave Egypt, they experience the miracle of the parting of the Sea of Reeds (or "Red Sea"); the giving of the Ten Commandments at Mount Sinai; the idolatry of the Golden Calf; and the design and construction of the Tabernacle and of the ark for the original tablets of the law, which our ancestors carried with them in the desert. Exodus also includes various ethical and civil laws, such as "You shall not wrong a stranger or oppress him, for you were strangers in the land of Egypt" (22:20).

> **Leviticus (about the Levites), or, in Hebrew, Va-yikra' (And God called).** It goes into great detail about the kinds of sacrifices that the ancient Israelites brought as offerings; the laws of ritual purity; the animals that were permitted and forbidden for eating (the beginnings of the tradition of kashrut, the Jewish dietary laws); the diagnosis of various skin diseases; the ethical laws of holiness; the ritual calendar of the Jewish year; and various agricultural laws concerning the treatment of the Land of Israel. Leviticus is basically the manual of ancient Judaism.

➤ Numbers (because the book begins with the census of the Israelites), or, in Hebrew, Be-midbar (In the wilderness). The book
describes the forty years of wandering in the wilderness and the
various rebellions against Moses. The constant theme: "Egypt
wasn't so bad. Maybe we should go back." The greatest rebellion
against Moses was the negative reports of the spies about the
Land of Israel, which discouraged the Israelites from wanting to
move forward into the land. For that reason, the "wilderness generation" must die off before a new generation can come into maturity and finish the journey.

➤ Deuteronomy (The repetition of the laws of the Torah), or, in
Hebrew, Devarim (The words). The final book of the Torah is,
essentially, Moses's farewell address to the Israelites as they pre-
pare to enter the Land of Israel. Here we find various laws that
had been previously taught, though sometimes with different
wording. Much of Deuteronomy contains laws that will be important to the Israelites as they enter the Land of Israel—laws
concerning the establishment of a monarchy and the ethics of
warfare. Perhaps the most famous passage from Deuteronomy
contains the *Shema,* the declaration of God's unity and unique-
ness, and the *Ve-ahavta,* which follows it. Deuteronomy ends with
the death of Moses on Mount Nebo as he looks across the Jordan
Valley into the land that he will not enter.

Jews read the Torah in sequence—starting with Bere'shit right after Simchat Torah in the autumn, and then finishing Devarim on the
following Simchat Torah. Each Torah portion is called a parashah (di-
vision; sometimes called a *sidrah,* a place in the order of the Torah
reading). The stories go around in a full circle, reminding us that we
can always gain more insights and more wisdom from the Torah. This
means that if you don't "get" the meaning this year, don't worry—it
will come around again.

And What Else? The Haftarah

We read or chant the Torah from the Torah scroll—the most sacred
thing that a Jewish community has in its possession. The Torah is

written without vowels, and the ability to read it and chant it is part of the challenge and the test.

But there is more to the synagogue reading. Every Torah reading has an accompanying haftarah reading. Haftarah means "conclusion," because there was once a time when the service actually ended with that reading. Some scholars believe that the reading of the haftarah originated at a time when non-Jewish authorities outlawed the reading of the Torah, and the Jews read the haftarah sections instead. In fact, in some synagogues, young people who become bar or bat mitzvah read very little Torah and instead read the entire haftarah portion.

The haftarah portion comes from the Nevi'im, the prophetic books, which are the second part of the Jewish Bible. It is either read or chanted from a Hebrew Bible, or maybe from a booklet or a photocopy.

The ancient sages chose the haftarah passages because their themes reminded them of the words or stories in the Torah text. Sometimes, they chose *haftarot* with special themes in honor of a festival or an upcoming festival.

Not all books in the prophetic section of the Hebrew Bible consist of prophecy. Several are historical. For example:

The book of Joshua tells the story of the conquest and settlement of Israel.

The book of Judges speaks of the period of early tribal rulers who would rise to power, usually for the purpose of uniting the tribes in war against their enemies. Some of these leaders are famous: Deborah, the great prophetess and military leader, and Samson, the biblical strong man.

The books of Samuel start with Samuel, the last judge, and then move to the creation of the Israelite monarchy under Saul and David (approximately 1000 BCE).

The books of Kings tell of the death of King David, the rise of King Solomon, and how the Israelite kingdom split into the Northern Kingdom of Israel and the Southern Kingdom of Judah (approximately 900 BCE).

And then there are the books of the prophets, those spokesmen for God whose words fired the Jewish conscience. Their names are immortal: Isaiah, Jeremiah, Ezekiel, Amos, Hosea, among others.

Someone once said: "There is no evidence of a biblical prophet ever being invited back a second time for dinner." Why? Because the prophets were tough. They had no patience for injustice, apathy, or hypocrisy. No one escaped their criticisms. Here's what they taught:

› God commands the Jews to behave decently toward one another. In fact, God cares more about basic ethics and decency than about ritual behavior.
› God chose the Jews *not* for special privileges, but for special duties to humanity.
› As bad as the Jews sometimes were, there was always the possibility that they would improve their behavior.
› As bad as things might be now, it will not always be that way. Someday, there will be universal justice and peace. Human history is moving forward toward an ultimate conclusion that some call the Messianic Age: a time of universal peace and prosperity for the Jewish people and for all the people of the world.

Your Mission—To Teach Torah to the Congregation

On the day when you become bar or bat mitzvah, you will be reading, or chanting, Torah—in Hebrew. You will be reading, or chanting, the haftarah—in Hebrew. That is the major skill that publicly marks the becoming of bar or bat mitzvah. But, perhaps even more important than that, you need to be able to teach something about the Torah portion, and perhaps the haftarah as well.

And that is where this book comes in. It will be a very valuable resource for you, and your family, in the b'nai mitzvah process.

Here is what you will find in it:

› A brief **summary** of every Torah portion. This is a basic overview of the portion; and, while it might not refer to everything in the Torah portion, it will explain its most important aspects.
› A list of the **major ideas** in the Torah portion. The purpose: to make the Torah portion real, in ways that we can relate to. Every Torah portion contains unique ideas, and when you put all

of those ideas together, you actually come up with a list of Judaism's most important ideas.

> Two *divrei Torah* ("words of Torah," or "sermonettes") for each portion. These *divrei Torah* explain significant aspects of the Torah portion in accessible, reader-friendly language. Each *devar Torah* contains references to **traditional** Jewish sources (those that were written before the modern era), as well as **modern** sources and quotes. We have searched, far and wide, to find sources that are unusual, interesting, and not just the "same old stuff" that many people already know about the Torah portion. Why did we include these minisermons in the volume? Not because we want you to simply copy those sermons and pass them off as your own (that would be cheating), though you are free to quote from them. We included them so that you can see what is possible—how you can try to make meaning for yourself out of the words of Torah.

> **Connections:** This is perhaps the most valuable part. It's a list of questions that you can ask yourself, or that others might help you think about—any of which can lead to the creation of your *devar Torah.*

Note: you don't have to like everything that's in a particular Torah portion. Some aren't that loveable. Some are hard to understand; some are about religious practices that people today might find confusing, and even offensive; some contain ideas that we might find totally outmoded.

But this doesn't have to get in the way. After all, most kids spend a lot of time thinking about stories that contain ideas that modern people would find totally bizarre. Any good medieval fantasy story falls into that category.

And we also believe that, if you spend just a little bit of time with those texts, you can begin to understand what the author was trying to say.

This volume goes one step further. Sometimes, the haftarah comes off as a second thought, and no one really thinks about it. We have tried to solve that problem by including a **summary** of each haftarah, and then a mini-sermon on the haftarah. This will help you learn how these sacred words are relevant to today's world, and even to your own life.

All Bible quotations come from the NJPS translation, which is found in the many different editions of the JPS TANAKH; in the Conservative movement's *Etz Hayim: Torah and Commentary;* in the Reform movement's *Torah: A Modern Commentary;* and in other Bible commentaries and study guides.

How Do I Write a *Devar Torah?*

It really is easier than it looks.

There are many ways of thinking about the *devar Torah.* It is, of course, a short sermon on the meaning of the Torah (and, perhaps, the haftarah) portion. It might even be helpful to think of the *devar Torah* as a "book report" on the portion itself.

The most important thing you can know about this sacred task is: *Learn* the words. *Love* the words. Teach people what it could mean to *live* the words.

Here's a basic outline for a *devar Torah:*

"My Torah portion is (name of portion) _____,
    from the book of _____ , chapter
    _____.
"In my Torah portion, we learn that_____
    (Summary of portion)
"For me, the most important lesson of this Torah portion is (what
    is the best thing in the portion? Take the portion as a whole;
    your *devar Torah* does not have to be only, or specifically, on the
    verses that you are reading).
"As I learned my Torah portion, I found myself wondering:
    ‣ *Raise a question that the Torah portion itself raises.*
    ‣ *"Pick a fight"* with the portion. Argue with it.
    ‣ *Answer a question* that is listed in the "Connections" section of
      each Torah portion.
    ‣ *Suggest a question to your rabbi* that you would want the rabbi
      to answer in his or her own *devar Torah* or sermon.

"I have lived the values of the Torah by _____
(here, you can talk about how the Torah portion relates to your
own life. If you have done a mitzvah project, you can talk about
that here).

How To Keep It from Being Boring
(and You from Being Bored)

Some people just don't like giving traditional speeches. From our per-
spective, that's really okay. Perhaps you can teach Torah in a different
way—one that makes sense to you.

> ▸ Write an "open letter" to one of the characters in your Torah por-
> tion. "Dear Abraham: I hope that your trip to Canaan was not too
> hard . . ." "Dear Moses: Were you afraid when you got the Ten
> Commandments on Mount Sinai? I sure would have been . . ."
> ▸ Write a news story about what happens. Imagine yourself to
> be a television or news reporter. "Residents of neighboring cit-
> ies were horrified yesterday as the wicked cities of Sodom and
> Gomorrah were burned to the ground. Some say that God was
> responsible . . ."
> ▸ Write an imaginary interview with a character in your Torah portion.
> ▸ Tell the story from the point of view of another character, or a mi-
> nor character, in the story. For instance, tell the story of the Gar-
> den of Eden from the point of view of the serpent. Or the story
> of the Binding of Isaac from the point of view of the ram, which
> was substituted for Isaac as a sacrifice. Or perhaps the story of
> the sale of Joseph from the point of view of his coat, which was
> stripped off him and dipped in a goat's blood.
> ▸ Write a poem about your Torah portion.
> ▸ Write a song about your Torah portion.
> ▸ Write a play about your Torah portion, and have some friends act
> it out with you.
> ▸ Create a piece of artwork about your Torah portion.

The bottom line is: Make this a joyful experience. Yes—it could
even be fun.

The Very Last Thing You Need to Know at This Point

The Torah scroll is written without vowels. Why? Don't *sofrim* (Torah scribes) know the vowels?

Of course they do.

So, why do they leave the vowels out?

One reason is that the Torah came into existence at a time when sages were still arguing about the proper vowels, and the proper pronunciation.

But here is another reason: The Torah text, as we have it today, and as it sits in the scroll, is actually *an unfinished work*. Think of it: the words are just sitting there. Because they have no vowels, it is as if they have no voice.

When we read the Torah publicly, we give voice to the ancient words. And when we find meaning in those ancient words, and we talk about those meanings, those words jump to life. They enter our lives. They make our world deeper and better.

Mazal tov to you, and your family. This is your journey toward Jewish maturity. Love it.

THE TORAH

❖ Metsora': Leviticus 14:1–15:33

You could call this portion Yuck Alert, Part 2 (or Part 3 or 4, but who's counting?). Metsora' is mostly concerned with that skin disease called *tzara'at*. But this portion is actually hopeful. It teaches about how the person who was afflicted with *tzara'at* and is now healed is reintegrated into the Israelite camp.

In last week's portion, we learned that this ailment could affect one's clothing (mildew). This week, however, it goes even further, telling us that it could even invade our houses.

Summary

> The priest is responsible for the rituals that accompany the reacceptance of the *metsora'* (the one afflicted with *tzara'at*) into the community. The sacrificial offerings that are mentioned are among the most elaborate and complicated in the entire Torah. (14:1–20)
> If the person who was afflicted cannot afford the "standard" sacrificial offerings, then he or she can bring "less expensive" offerings: one lamb, flour, oil, or turtledoves or pigeons. (14:21–32)
> *Tzara'at* could show up on the bricks of a house. Today, we would refer to this as "mold." (14:34–57)

The Big Ideas

> **The priest's role is not only to deal with ritual.** Biblical Judaism
> had a very big sense of the priestly role. It was not only to offer
> sacrifices, but also to pay attention to the health of the Israelites
> and be part of the healing process for those who were ill. People
> with *tzara'at* were removed from the community (probably be-
> cause of the fear of contagion), but they had to be accepted back
> in when they were healed.

> **Judaism is for the poor, as well as for those who are more pros-
> perous.** The person who suffers from *tzara'at* did not have to
> bring an elaborate sacrifice if he or she could not afford it. Other
> arrangements were made. Judaism is not only for the prosperous;
> the poor also have dignity and the ability to serve God.

> **Impurity can affect our homes.** Because the home is one's per-
> sonal domain, we have to make sure that the various "illnesses"
> that are part of the outside world are prevented from entering
> these holy spaces of our lives.

Divrei Torah

WE DON'T HAVE ALL THE ANSWERS

In our Torah portion, it says that a plague of *tzara'at* could come into your house (14:34). We would call that mold, and no doubt about it—it is nasty. When it gets into a house, it can make the inhabitants sick. Bad stuff.

But here's the intriguing part back in biblical times: the person who owned the house had to come to the priest to report the problem. In that sense, the priest was like a public health official. And the homeowner had to say: "*K'nega nireh li ba-bayit*"—roughly translated, "Something like a plague, it appears to me, is in the house."

The homeowner didn't go to the priest and say: "Excuse me, Mr. Kohen [priest], you need to come. There is a plague in my house!" He was to say it in a much softer tone: "It appears to me that there is something like a plague in my house." The person may be sure that the plague has struck, but is instructed not to say it that way.

Why was that? Because it was the job of the priest, not the homeowner, to determine if there was something going on in the house, and to take the steps to correct it. The priest was the expert.

We often think that we are the experts and that we know it all. We may be right; we may be wrong, but that is not the point. Rabbi Eliyahu Mizrahi, a Turkish sage of the fifteenth century, writes: "This serves as a moral lesson. Even in the event of certainty about an impurity, one should declare it as doubtful. Thus our sages have stated, 'Teach your tongue to say, "I do not know."'"

The Torah is trying to teach us a very important value—humility. While we are tempted to boast about the things we know, it is much more important to be tentative about the things we don't know. Sometimes that can be hard to admit, especially when it might appear that we are not as knowledgeable or competent as we think we should be.

Rabbi Gil Steinlauf has written: "I love not knowing! When people come up to me and ask me a question about Judaism—or anything—I'm happy to admit when I don't know the answer. I'm grateful. That person has given me an opportunity to look something up and to learn. How else can I find the Truth? How else can I be ultimately right?"

It is humbling, and so liberating to admit that you don't have all the answers.

GOSSIP IS CONTAGIOUS

Nowadays when people get sick they assume that it's because of germs, or viruses, or just bad luck. Even when people get sick as a direct or indirect result of something that they might have done (like smoking cigarettes), we wouldn't bring those underlying reasons up as part of the conversation. Too cruel. Unnecessary.

But back in ancient times when people got sick, they often thought that it was because of something they had done; they thought that it was direct punishment for moral sins. Knowing that, it's not surprising to learn the ancient sages' response to why people got afflicted with *tzara'at*. They took the word for the one who is afflicted—*metsora'*—and turned it into a pun. They said that the *metsora'* is the person who is *motzi ra*, someone who says bad things about other people.

So you could say that a *motzi ra* is a gossip. In Hebrew, there are numerous words for this kind of sin—for example, *lashon ha-ra* (the evil tongue) or *rekhilut* (tale bearing). And for Jews this is a very big deal. Look how many sins in the High Holy Day prayer book refer to sins of the mouth. "For the sin we have committed against God by gossip, and by tale-bearing, and by mocking and scoffing, and by falsehood, and by needlessly judging other people."

Lashon ha-ra means saying anything bad about anyone, even and especially if it's true. *Lashon ha-ra* means insults, ridicule, and jest, and denigrating someone's possessions, or work, or merchandise. It means commenting on someone's body, mind, money, or medical history; saying anything that might cause another person harm, embarrassment, or displeasure. "Did you hear what he did?" "Did you hear what she said?" "I heard that he actually . . ." "I really shouldn't say, but . . ."

Language is a very powerful thing; it has within it the power of life and death. According to the Talmud, to shame another person in public is tantamount to shedding blood. God created the world through language. God said, "Let there be light, and there was light" (Gen. 1:3).

Rabbi Judah Loew of sixteenth-century Prague was the creator of the Golem, the famous Jewish "Frankenstein" who protected the

Jews from their enemies. Rabbi Loew taught: "Consider the Hebrew word for language, *lashon.* The first letter, *lamed,* points upward—to remind us that language can bring us to the heavens. But the last letter, *nun,* points downward—to remind us that language can sink us into the abyss."

Gossip doesn't only exist in verbal form. It exists in social media, where it can spread even faster than a biblical contagious disease. Whenever you hear gossip about someone, turn the conversation around to other things. Just say: "Let's talk about something else." Gossip may not cause you to get a skin disease, but it can do plenty of damage. And it is contagious!

Connections

- What lessons can we learn from people who think they know it all?
- What are some things that you don't know about and would be curious to learn about?
- When have you admitted that you were wrong about something? What does it feel like?
- Can you think of times when people have been hurt by gossip?
- What can you do to prevent yourself and others you know from gossiping?

THE HAFTAROT

❖ Metsora': 2 Kings 7:3–20

To be Jewish means to be have hope. And here is why.

In this haftarah the Northern Kingdom of Israel (also known as Samaria) is at war with Syria (also known as Aram). The conditions are terrible. A famine breaks out that is so severe that people actually resort to cannibalism. Four Israelite lepers (leprosy, or some kind of skin disease, is the connection to the Torah portion) are sitting outside the gates of Samaria. They believe that they are on the verge of death, and so they decide to go over to the Arameans—after all, they have nothing to lose. When they get to the Aramean camp, they find it deserted, because God had frightened the soldiers away.

The lepers find enough provisions in the Aramean camp to feed and equip themselves and others in Samaria. The Israelite army goes out and finds supplies that the Aramean army has left by the side of the road, and they bring these things into the Israelite camp.

The prophet Elisha ("the man of God," 7:18) had prophesized that there would be enough food for everyone, and that the price of barley and flour would therefore come down. An officer expressed his doubts about that happening. But it did, and people rushed out of the city of Samaria for the food—and in the process, trampled the officer to death.

The moral of the story: don't lose hope; things can always get better.

We Will Survive!

Call it a coincidence if you want, but this Torah portion and its accompanying haftarah often appear right around Yom ha-Shoah (the commemoration of the Holocaust), or sometimes a week later, at Yom ha-Atzmaut (Israel Independence Day).

So, even though you might find the whole topic of leprosy, or *tzara'at*, to be profoundly unappealing, pay attention. There is much that we can learn.

Think back to Samaria at the time that this haftarah takes place. Consider the conditions there. The Samarians are at war. People are starving. And then this group of four lepers—who are already the lowest of the low, because lepers were always ostracized from society—take a look at each other and say, in essence: "Just what are we doing here? Yes, we might die. But why should we wait for death? Let's do something outrageous. Let's join the Arameans!"

An act of treason? Probably. Admirable? Probably not. An act of desperation? You bet. The point is: they refuse to simply sit around and die. They have to do something. And they do. And luckily for them, God had scared the daylights out of the Aramean army, who had run away and left all their stuff behind, and the famine lifted.

And what does this have to do with Yom ha-Shoah, or Yom ha-Atzmaut?

Imagine what those four lepers looked like. Pretty bad, right? Actually, probably pretty gruesome—emaciated, with their skin peeling? That is exactly what the survivors of the Shoah, the Holocaust, were like. And like the people of ancient Samaria, they had managed to survive. True: unlike the lepers in our story, none of them went over to the German army. But here's the major point: they refused to die. They refused to give up hope. They believed that they could live again and make new lives. And that is precisely what they did.

The modern Jewish thinker Emil Fackenheim said: "We are forbidden to hand Hitler any posthumous victories." What he meant was that Jews have to maintain hope and keep on living. That is what the Jews did after the Shoah, and because of that faith in life the State of Israel came into being. Remember the national anthem of the Jewish people— "Hatikvah" (The hope), which says "Our hope is not yet lost—the hope of two thousand years. To be a free people in our land, in Zion, and in Jerusalem."

The book of Job expresses this hope in another way, comparing us to trees that are cut down but survive because of their roots. "There is hope for a tree; if it is cut down it will renew itself; its shoots will not cease. If its roots are old in the earth, and its stump dies in the ground, at the scent of water it will bud and produce branches like a sapling" (Job 14: 7–9). Life may cut us down; but hope springs eternal.

❖ Notes

❖ Notes

CPSIA information can be obtained
at www.ICGtesting.com
Printed in the USA
LVHW091625011218
598911LV00001B/66/P

9 780827 614130